THIS BOOK BELONGS TO

STERLING TEEN and the distinctive
Sterling Teen logo are registered trademarks of
Sterling Publishing Co., Inc.

First Sterling edition published in 2021.

ISBN: 978-1-4549-4385-3

Distributed in Canada by Sterling Publishing Co., Inc. c/o Canadian Manda Group,664 Annette Street, Toronto,Ontario M6S 2C8, Canada

For information about custom editions, special sales, and premium and corporate purchases, please contact Sterling Special Sales at 800–805–5489 or specialsales@sterlingpublishing.com.

Manufactured in Singapore

2 4 6 8 10 9 7 5 3 1

08/21

sterlingpublishing.com

Color my mood

A Cute Activity Journal for Tracking My Feelings

Olive Yong, Creator of Bichi Mao

STERLING TEEN
New York

MEET OLIVE!

A.K.A. THE CREATOR OF BICHI MAO

Hi, my name is Olive Yong.

I'm a self-taught artist from Malaysia. Drawing has always been a passion of mine, and I am proud to share my book with you! *Color My Mood*, in all its kawaii glory, has been so much fun to illustrate.

My aim is to spread positivity and make people smile. I often receive messages or emails from my followers telling me how my comics have impacted their life, and that always brings a smile to my face and I know all my hard work is worth it. I will never stop creating and spreading the love. Thank you to those who have always supported my passion for creating and kept believing in me.

I'm grateful that I persevered and did not give up. W. Clement Stone once said, *"Aim for the moon. If you miss, you may hit a star."*

ABOUT THE AUTHOR

In 2019, Olive began to post her art across social media platforms under the brand name Bichi Mao. Bichi Mao is a slice-of-life webcomic series revolving around cat characters presented in an adorable and simplistic art style. The comics are gentle and playful, with moments that tug at the heartstrings when you least expect them to.

Within a year of Olive's early posts, Bichi Mao gained a large following. Olive was surprised and delighted that so many people liked what she was doing, and she was encouraged to continue. The support she receives means the world to her and drives her to continue creating and drawing.

ABOUT THIS BOOK

Ever feel like you're on autopilot sometimes? Are you surprised by things you do, say, think, or feel, and then wonder where your tears and temper tantrums came from?

If your life is filled with clouds and it seems the super-computer between your ears has been pre-programed with secret software that can turn itself on and off whenever it wants, making you feel all sorts of ups and downs—fear not young grasshopper!

Even if you're not in the mood, all it takes is 10 seconds a day to color the carrots and candies, open your heart and mind, and become who you want to be.

WHY TRACK YOUR MOOD?

Tracking your moods will reveal patterns that, once understood, will quickly illuminate and enrich your life. By contemplating and connecting the dots, it will become obvious to you how your moods are at the helm and are steering your ship through your weeks, months, and years.

Tuning in to your gut feelings and emotional reactions will give you superpowers, allowing you to turn old habits into new choices. Think of this mood-tracking companion as a safe place to express your thoughts and feelings, and treat it like a map leading to the treasure hiding inside you. Remember: the more you use it, the more clues you will get about where to dig!

YOU WILL NEED

Something to color with. Rustle up some pencils, crayons, or marker pens. And whether you believe communicating with your inner self is a science experiment or a spiritual practice, a spirit of adventure will serve you well (along with a willingness to not only articulate how you feel, but also carefully reflect on the patterns you see).

FILL IN THE BLANKS

1. When to start: You can start the 5-year journal in any calendar month and on any day in the month. No need to wait for the start of the year or the beginning of a month—just dive right in. Keep this book beside your bed in a special place. Find a time toward the end of the day, maybe just before you go to sleep, when you can have a few moments to reflect on how you're feeling.

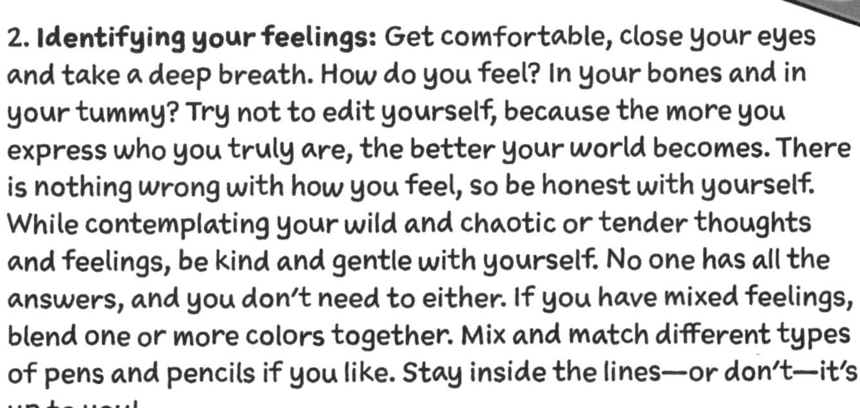

2. Identifying your feelings: Get comfortable, close your eyes and take a deep breath. How do you feel? In your bones and in your tummy? Try not to edit yourself, because the more you express who you truly are, the better your world becomes. There is nothing wrong with how you feel, so be honest with yourself. While contemplating your wild and chaotic or tender thoughts and feelings, be kind and gentle with yourself. No one has all the answers, and you don't need to either. If you have mixed feelings, blend one or more colors together. Mix and match different types of pens and pencils if you like. Stay inside the lines—or don't—it's up to you!

3. Angry? Happy? OK? Sad? As you begin each month, color in the mood key. Let different colors reflect your evolving objective perspective. Maybe yellow indicates "happy" this month, but "OK"

next month, while blue signifies "sad" this month, and "angry" next month. (We've deliberately provided only four mood options to make it easier to help you identify what you are feeling.) Choose one of these mood options and use the allocated color to shade in the relevant day on the artwork on the page opposite. It will take about 10 seconds. There! Now you have a record of how you are feeling today.

4. Come back tomorrow: Make sure to come back here at least once a day and let your feelings flow.

LOOKING BACK

Pay attention to the patterns you see. What do the multicolored dinosaur fins, popcorn kernels, and shooting stars have to say? What moody mysteries did the bananas, birds, and butterflies reveal to you?

On the last day of every month (or year, if you prefer—this is a 5-year journal after all) ask yourself: Overall, how did I feel? Did my feelings cause me to do things I was proud of or that I later regretted? See if you can notice the influence that other people, holidays, or events had (or are having) on your moods at different times of the month (or year).

Remember that light-hearted joy is hiding inside the micro-second moments of your moods—every single day—just waiting to show up when you acknowledge and appreciate the rhythm and rhyme of your innermost feelings.

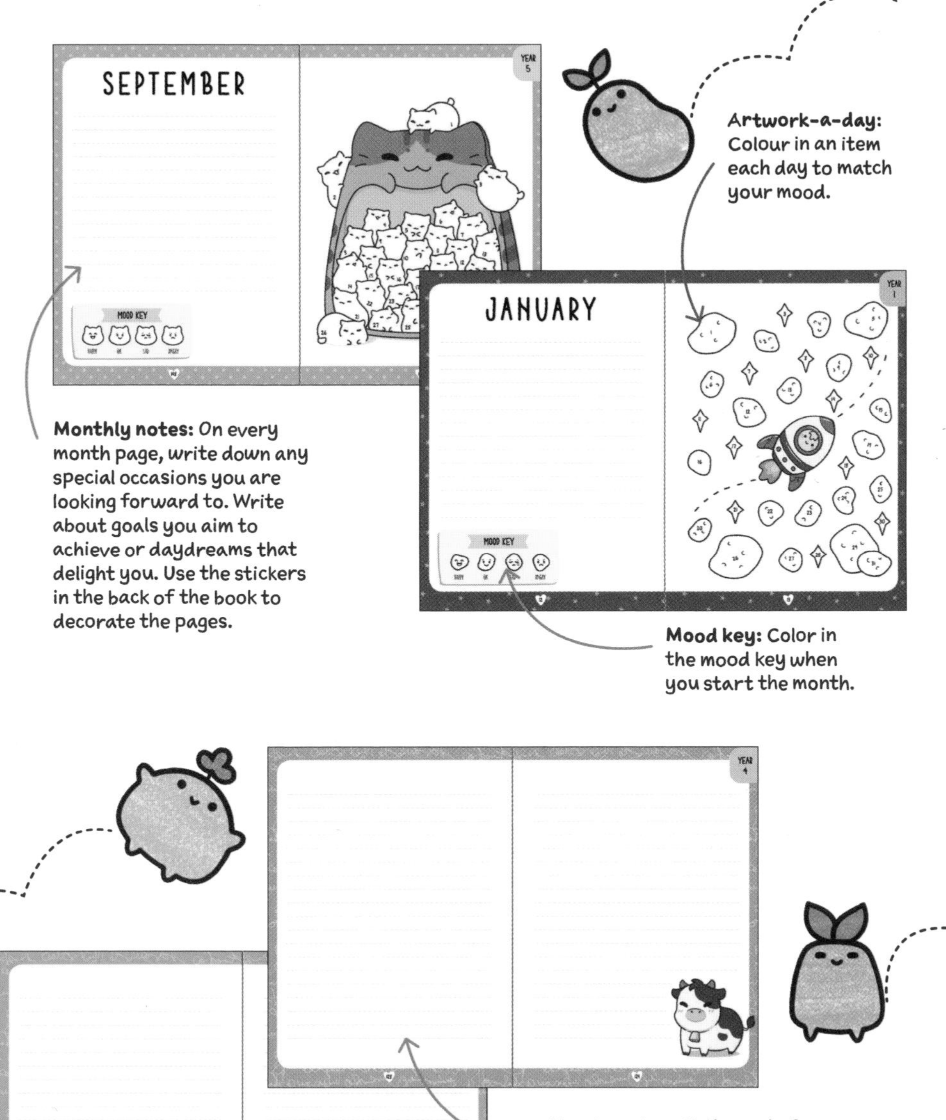

Artwork-a-day: Colour in an item each day to match your mood.

Monthly notes: On every month page, write down any special occasions you are looking forward to. Write about goals you aim to achieve or daydreams that delight you. Use the stickers in the back of the book to decorate the pages.

Mood key: Color in the mood key when you start the month.

Yearly notes: At the end of every year, you will find four pages for you to fill as you please. This might be a reflection of the year, or you might use it to document a special trip or moment. Use the stickers in the back of the book to decorate the pages.

MY GOALS FOR THE YEAR

YEAR 1

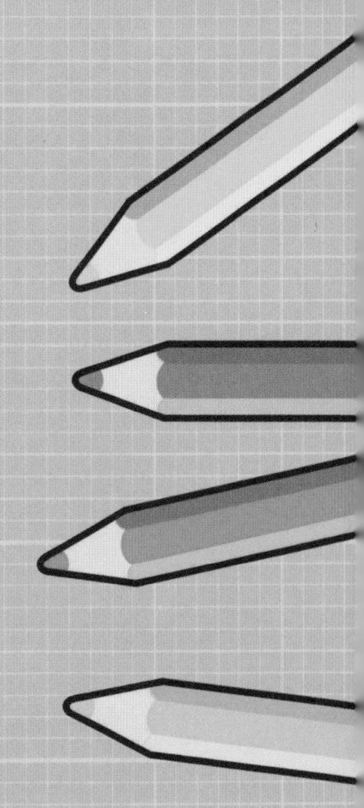

JANUARY

MOOD KEY

HAPPY

OK

SAD

ANGRY

1
2
3
4
5
6
7
8
9
10
11
12
13
14
15
16
17
18
19
20
21
22
23
24
25
26
27
28
29
30
31

FEBRUARY

MOOD KEY

HAPPY

OK

SAD

ANGRY

Love
1
2
3
4
5
6
7
8
9
10
11
12
13
14
15
16
17
18
19
20
21
22
23
24
25
26
27
28
29

MARCH

1
2
3
4
5
6
7
8
9
10
11
12
13
14
15
16
17
18
19
20
21
22
23
24
25
26
27
28
29
30
31

APRIL

1
2
3
4
5
6
7
8
9
10
11
12
13
14
15
16
17
18
19
20
21
22
23
24
25
26
27
28
29
30

MAY

MOOD KEY

HAPPY OK SAD ANGRY

1
2
3
4
5
6
7
8
9
10
11
12
13
14
15
16
17
18
19
20
21
22
23
24
25
26
27
28
29
30
31

JUNE

1
2
3
4
5
6
7
8
9
10
11
12
13
14
15
16
17
18
19
20
21
22
23
24
25
26
27
28
29
30

JULY

MOOD KEY

HAPPY OK SAD ANGRY

1
2
3
4
5
6
7
8
9
10
11
12
13
14
15
16
17
18
19
20
21
22
23
24
25
26
27
28
29
30
31

AUGUST

1
2
3
4
5
6
7
8
9
10
11
12
13
14
15
16
17
18
19
20
21
22
23
24
25
26
27
28
29
30
31
SMILE

SEPTEMBER

MOOD KEY

HAPPY OK SAD ANGRY

4
1
2
3
5
6
8
10
11
7
15
9
12
16
17
13
14
21
18
20
22
23
19
24
27
28
30
25
26
29

OCTOBER

MOOD KEY

HAPPY OK SAD ANGRY

1
2
3
4
5
6
7
8
9
10
11
12
13
14
15
16
17
18
19
20
21
22
23
24
25
26
27
28
29
30
31

NOVEMBER

1
2
3
4
5
6
7
8
9
10
11
12
13
14
15
16
17
18
19
20
21
22
23
24
25
26
27
28
29
30

DECEMBER

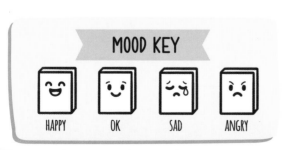

MOOD KEY

HAPPY OK SAD ANGRY

1
2
3
4
5
6
7
8
9
10
11
12
13
14
15
16
17
18
19
20
21
22
23
24
25
26
27
28
29
30
31

MY GOALS FOR THE YEAR

YEAR 2

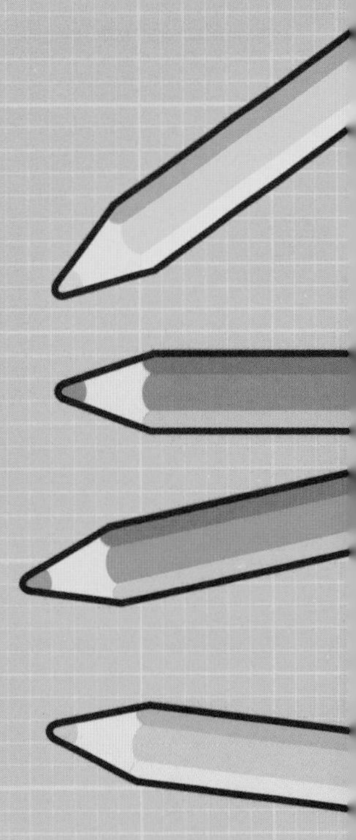

JANUARY

1
2
3
4
5
6
7
8
9
10
11
12
13
14
15
16
17
18
19
20
21
22
23
24
25
26
27
28
29
30
31

FEBRUARY

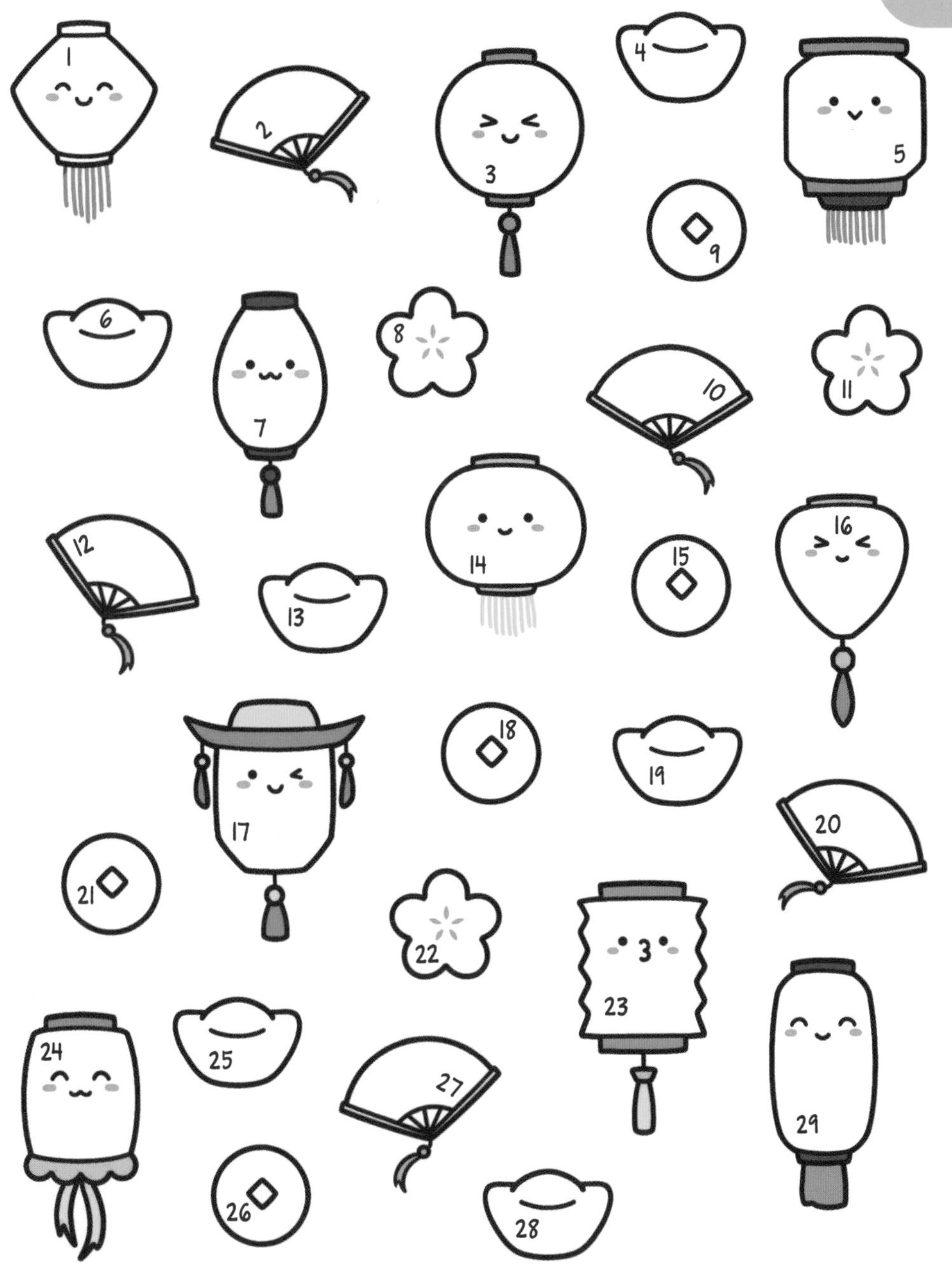
1
2
3
4
5
9
6
7
8
10
11
12
13
14
15
16
17
18
19
20
21
22
23
24
25
27
26
28
29

MARCH

MOOD KEY

HAPPY

OK

SAD

ANGRY

1
2
3
4
5
6
7
8
9
10
11
12
13
14
15
16
17
18
19
20
21
22
23
24
25
26
27
28
29
30
31

APRIL

MOOD KEY

HAPPY OK SAD ANGRY

1
2
3
4
5
6
7
8
9
10
11
12
13
14
15
16
17
18
19
20
21
22
23
24
25
26
27
28
29
30

MAY

1
2
3
4
5
6
7
8
9
10
11
12
13
14
15
16
17
18
19
20
21
22
23
24
25
26
27
28
29
30
31

JUNE

1
2
3
4
5
6
7
8
9
10
11
12
13
14
15
16
17
18
19
20
21
22
23
24
25
26
27
28
29
30

JULY

MOOD KEY

HAPPY

OK

SAD

ANGRY

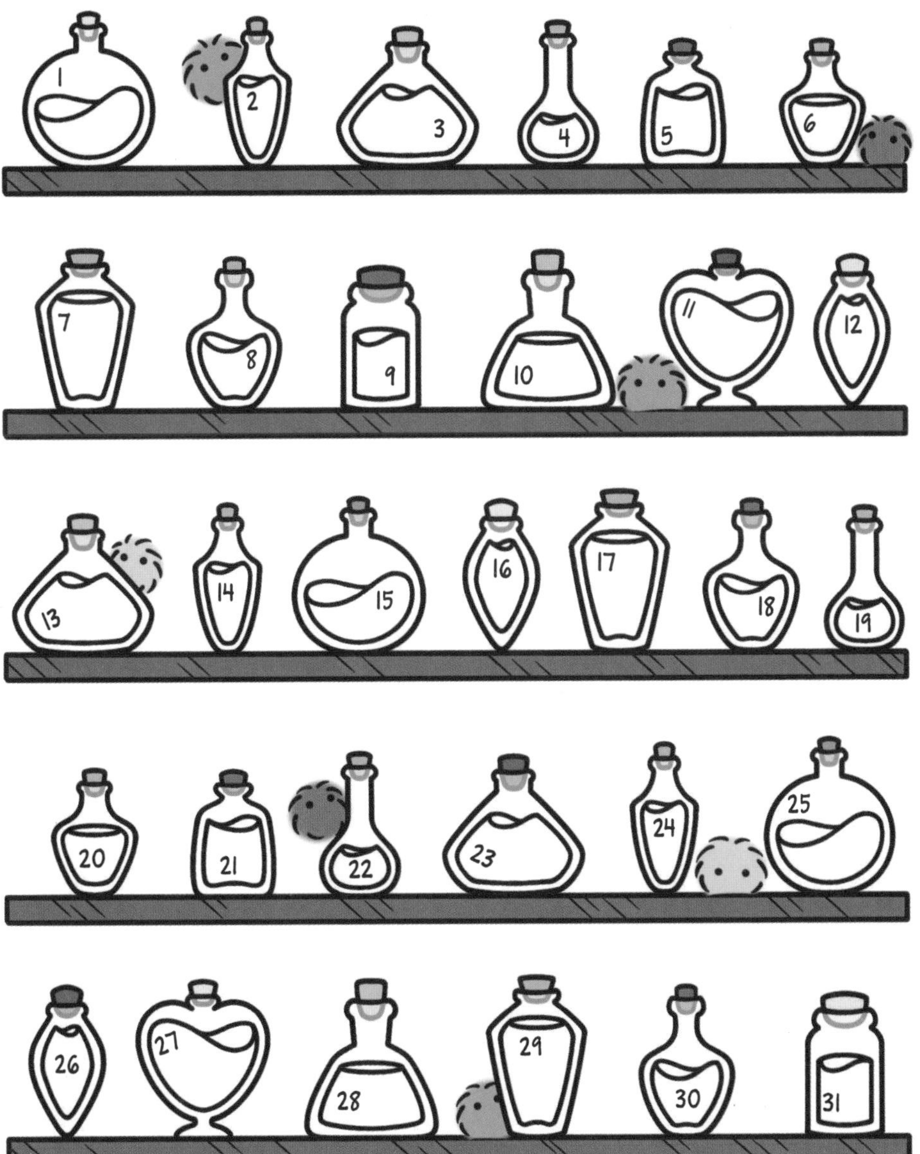
1
2
3
4
5
6
7
8
9
10
11
12
13
14
15
16
17
18
19
20
21
22
23
24
25
26
27
28
29
30
31

AUGUST

MOOD KEY

HAPPY OK SAD ANGRY

1
2
3
4
5
6
7
8
9
10
11
12
13
14
15
16
17
Honey
18
19
20
21
22
23
24
25
26
27
28
29
30
31

SEPTEMBER

1
2
3
4
5
6
7
8
9
10
11
12
13
14
15
16
17
18
19
20
21
22
23
24
25
26
27
28
29
30

OCTOBER

MOOD KEY

HAPPY OK SAD ANGRY

1
2
3
4
5
6
7
8
9
10
11
12
13
14
15
16
17
18
19
20
21
22
23
24
25
26
27
28
29
30
31

NOVEMBER

1
2
3
4
5
6
7
8
9
10
11
12
13
14
15
16
17
18
19
20
21
22
23
24
25
26
27
28
29
30

DECEMBER

MOOD KEY

HAPPY OK SAD ANGRY

1 2 3 4 5 6 7 8 9 10 11 12 13 14 15 16 17 18 19 20 21 22 23 24 25 26 27 28 29 30 31

Honey

MY GOALS FOR THE YEAR

YEAR 3

JANUARY

1
2
3
4
5
6
7
8
9
10
11
12
13
14
15
16
17
18
19
20
21
22
23
24
25
26
27
28
29
30
31

FEBRUARY

1
2
3
4
5
6
7
8
9
10
11
12
13
14
15
16
17
18
19
20
21
22
23
24
25
26
27
28
29

MARCH

TICKET
1
2
3
4
5
6
7
8
9
10
11
12
13
14
15
16
17
18
19
20
21
22
23
23
24
25
26
27
28
29
30
31

APRIL

1
2
3
4
5
6
7
8
9
10
11
12
13
14
15
16
17
18
19
20
21
22
23
24
25
26
27
28
29
30

MAY

MOOD KEY

HAPPY

OK

SAD

ANGRY

1
2
3
4
6
7
5
3
9
8
14
12
13
3
10
11
19
17
15
3
16
18
21
23
20
22
24
27
30
25
31
26
28
29

JUNE

MOOD KEY

HAPPY OK SAD ANGRY

1
2
3
4
5
6
7
8
9
10
11
12
13
14
15
16
17
18
19
20
21
22
23
24
25
26
27
28
29
30

JULY

MOOD KEY

HAPPY OK SAD ANGRY

1
2
3
4
5
6
7
8
9
10
11
12
13
14
15
16
17
18
19
20
21
22
23
24
25
26
27
28
29
30
31

AUGUST

1
2
3
4
5
6
7
8
9
10
11
12
13
14
15
16
17
18
19
20
21
22
23
24
25
26
27
28
29
30
31

SEPTEMBER

1
2
3
4
5
6
7
8
9
10
11
12
13
14
15
16
17
18
19
20
21
22
23
24
25
26
27
28
29
30

OCTOBER

MOOD KEY

HAPPY OK SAD ANGRY

1
2
3
4
5
6
7
8
9
10
11
12
13
14
15
16
17
18
19
20
21
22
23
24
25
26
27
28
29
30
31

NOVEMBER

1
2
3
4
5
6
7
8
9
10
11
12
13
14
15
16
17
18
19
20
21
22
23
24
25
26
27
28
29
30

DECEMBER

MOOD KEY

HAPPY OK SAD ANGRY

1
2
3
4
5
6
7
8
9
10
11
12
13
14
15
16
17
18
19
20
21
22
23
24
25
26
27
28
29
30
31

MY GOALS FOR THE YEAR

YEAR 4

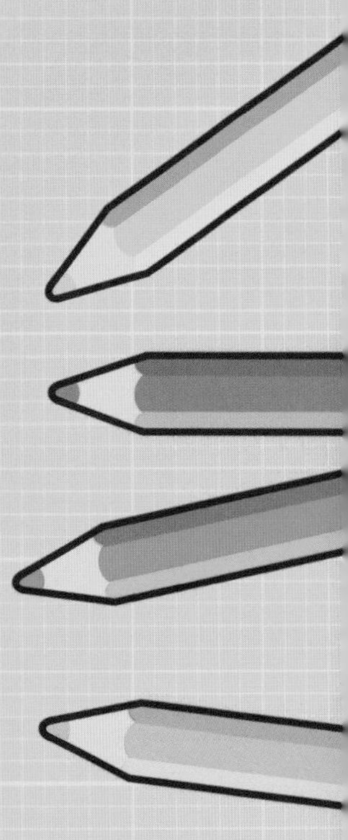

JANUARY

MOOD KEY

HAPPY OK SAD ANGRY

1
2
3
4
5
6
7
8
9
10
11
12
13
14
15
16
17
18
19
20
21
22
23
24
25
26
27
28
29
30
31

FEBRUARY

1
2
3
4
5
6
7
8
9
10
11
12
13
14
15
16
17
18
19
20
21
22
23
24
25
26
27
28
29

MARCH

1
2
3
4
5
6
7
8
9
10
11
12
13
14
15
16
17
18
19
20
21
22
23
24
25
26
27
28
29
30
31

APRIL

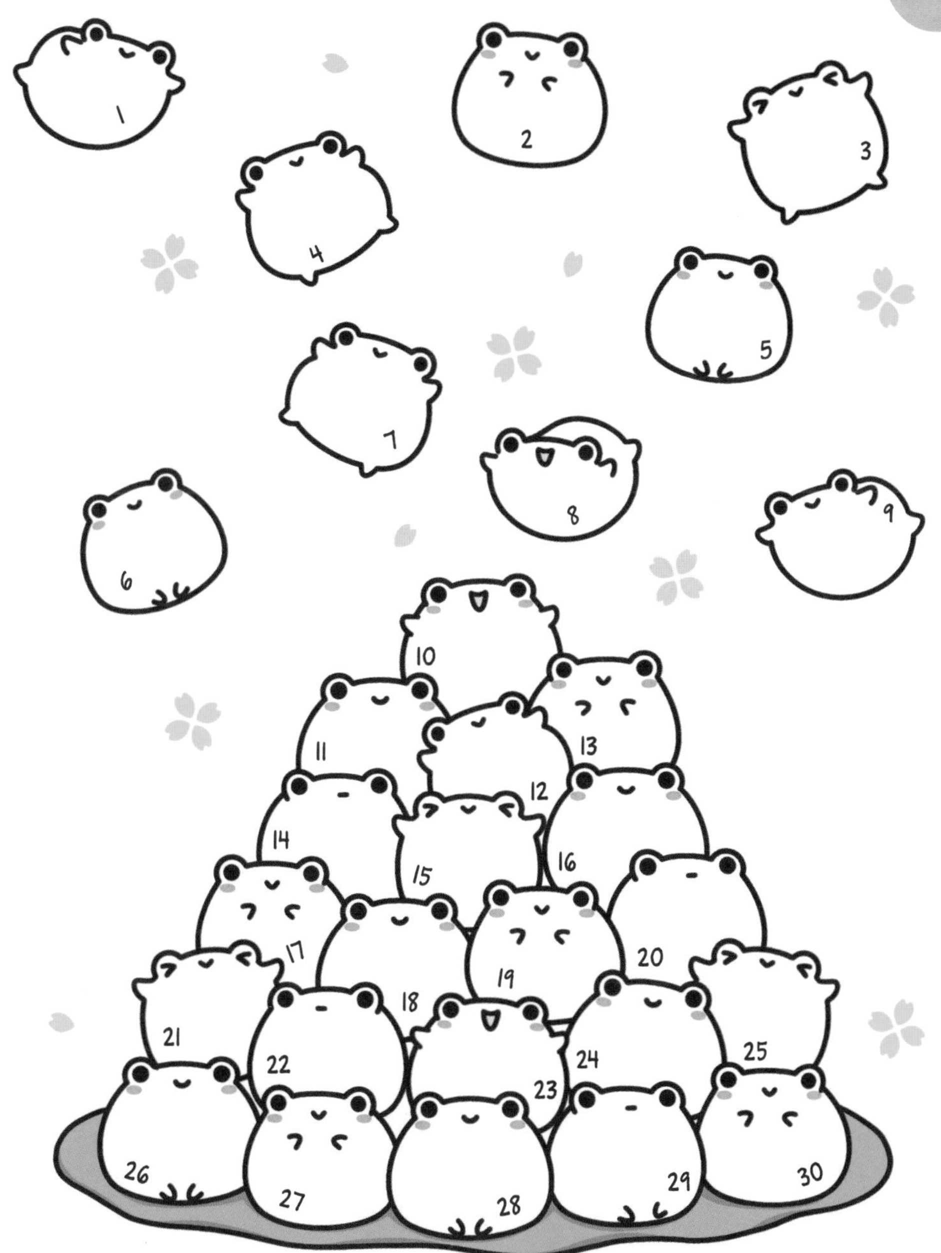
1
2
3
4
5
6
7
8
9
10
11
12
13
14
15
16
17
18
19
20
21
22
23
24
25
26
27
28
29
30

MAY

Mango Candy
1
2
3
4
5
6
7
8
9
10
11
12
13
14
15
16
17
18
19
20
21
22
23
24
25
26
27
28
29
30
31

JUNE

MOOD KEY

HAPPY OK SAD ANGRY

1
2
3
4
5
6
7
8
9
10
11
12
13
14
15
16
17
18
19
20
21
22
23
24
25
26
27
28
29
30

JULY

MOOD KEY

HAPPY OK SAD ANGRY

2
1
8
3
4
5
6
9
11
7
10
14
16
12
13
15
17
20
21
19
18
23
25
22
24
26
28
27
29
30
31
31

AUGUST

MOOD KEY

HAPPY OK SAD ANGRY

1
2
3
4
5
6
7
8
9
10
11
12
13
14
15
16
17
18
19
20
21
22
23
24
25
26
27
28
29
30
31

SEPTEMBER

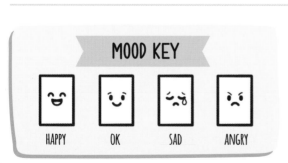

MOOD KEY

HAPPY OK SAD ANGRY

1
2
3
4
5
6
7
8
9
10
11
12
13
14
15
16
17
18
19
20
21
22
23
24
25
26
27
28
29
30

OCTOBER

MOOD KEY

HAPPY

OK

SAD

ANGRY

1
2
3
4
5
6
7
8
9
10
11
12
13
14
15
16
17
18
19
20
21
22
23
24
25
26
27
28
29
30
31

NOVEMBER

1
2
3
4
5
6
7
8
9
10
11
12
13
14
15
16
17
18
19
20
21
22
23
24
25
26
27
28
29
30

DECEMBER

1
2
3
4
5
6
7
8
9
10
11
12
13
14
15
16
17
18
19
20
21
22
23
24
25
26
27
28
29
30
31

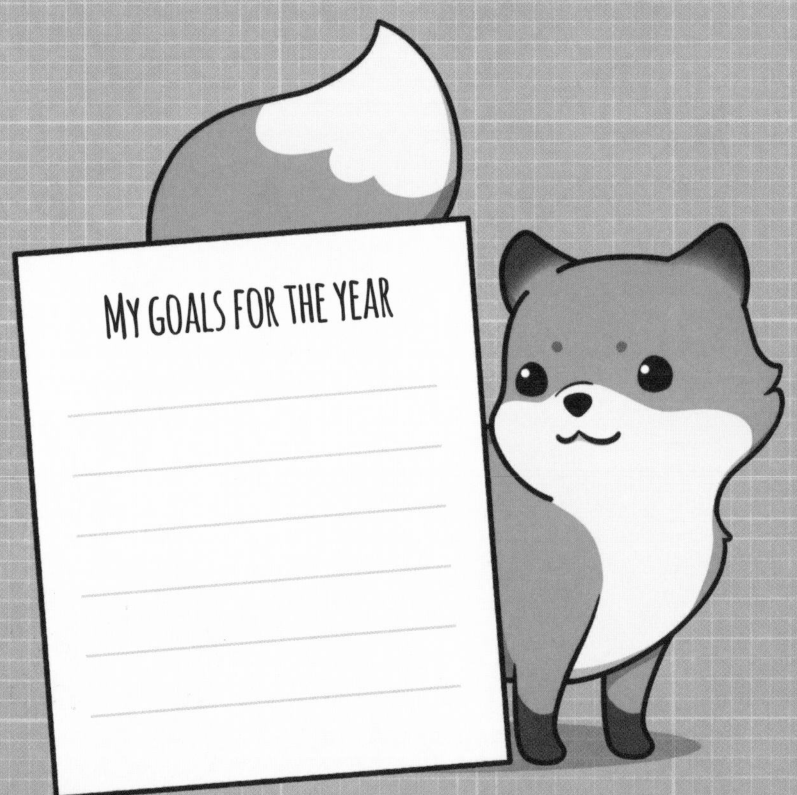
MY GOALS FOR THE YEAR

YEAR 5

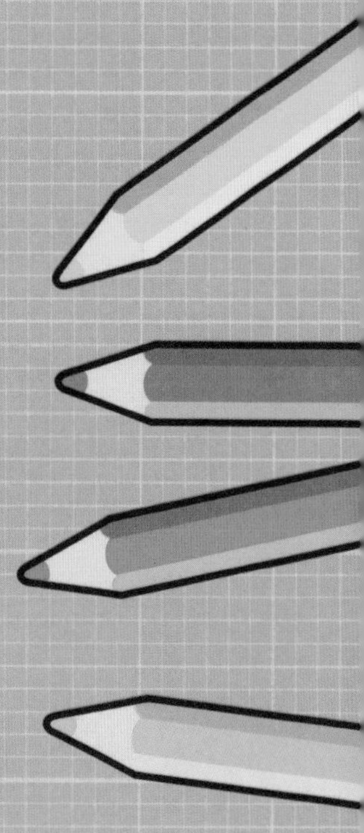

JANUARY

1
2
3
4
5
6
7
8
9
10
11
12
13
14
15
16
17
18
19
20
21
22
23
24
25
26
27
28
29
30
31

FEBRUARY

1
2
3
4
5
6
7
8
9
10
11
12
13
14
15
16
17
18
19
20
21
22
23
24
25
26
27
28
29

MARCH

1
2
3
4
5
6
7
8
9
10
11
12
13
14
15
16
17
18
19
20
21
22
23
24
25
26
27
28
29
30
31

APRIL

1
2
3
4
5
6
7
8
9
10
11
12
13
14
15
16
17
18
19
20
21
22
23
24
25
26
27
28
29
30

MAY

MOOD KEY

HAPPY OK SAD ANGRY

1
2
3
4
5
6
7
8
9
10
11
12
13
14
15
16
17
18
19
20
21
22
23
24
25
26
27
28
29
30
31

JUNE

MOOD KEY

HAPPY OK SAD ANGRY

1
2
3
4
5
6
7
8
9
10
11
12
13
14
15
16
17
18
19
20
21
22
23
24
25
26
27
28
29
30

JULY

MOOD KEY

HAPPY

OK

SAD

ANGRY

1
2
3
4
5
6
7
8
9
10
11
12
13
14
15
16
17
18
19
20
21
22
23
24
25
26
27
28
29
30
31

AUGUST

MOOD KEY

HAPPY OK SAD ANGRY

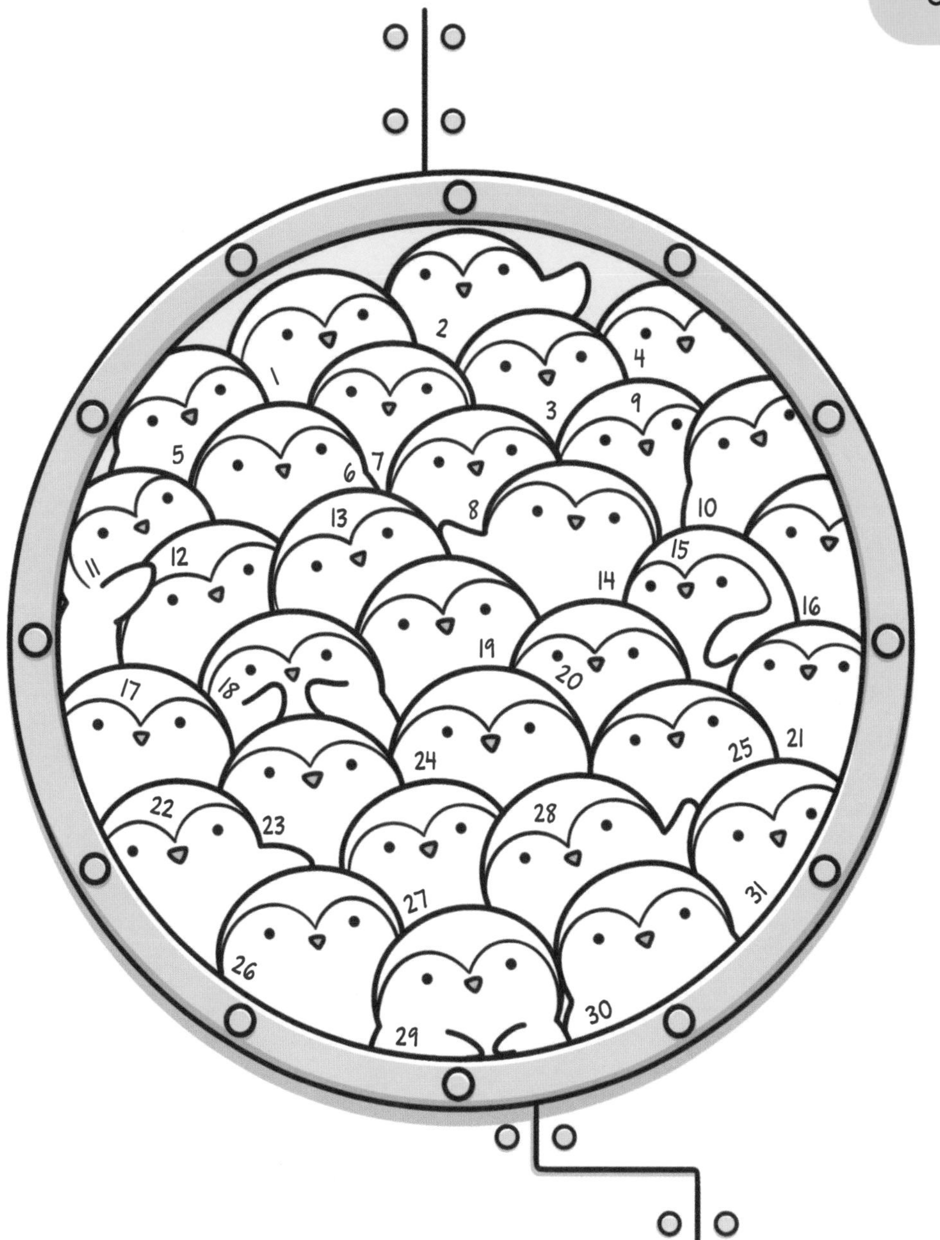
1
2
3
4
5
6
7
8
9
10
11
12
13
14
15
16
17
18
19
20
21
22
23
24
25
26
27
28
29
30
31

SEPTEMBER

MOOD KEY

HAPPY OK SAD ANGRY

1
2
3
4
5
6
7
8
9
10
11
12
13
14
15
16
17
18
19
20
21
22
23
24
25
26
27
28
29
30

OCTOBER

1
2
3
4
5
6
7
8
9
10
11
12
13
14
15
16
17
18
19
20
21
22
23
24
25
26
27
28
29
30
31

NOVEMBER

MOOD KEY

HAPPY

OK

SAD

ANGRY

1
2
3
4
5
6
7
8
9
10
11
12
13
14
15
16
17
18
19
20
21
22
23
24
25
26
27
28
29
30

DECEMBER

MOOD KEY

HAPPY OK SAD ANGRY

1
2
3
4
5
6
7
8
9
10
11
12
13
14
15
16
17
18
19
20
21
22
23
24
25
26
27
28
29
30
31